First German

ON HOLIDAY

Kathy Gemmell and Jenny Tyler
Illustrated by Sue Stitt
Designed by Diane Thistlethwaite

Consultant: Sandy Walker

CONTENTS

First published in 1993 by Usborne Publishing Ltd.
Usborne House, 83-85 Saffron Hill,
London EC1N 8RT, England.
Copyright © 1993 Usborne Publishing Ltd.

2 Printed in Portugal. UE

Speaking German

This book is about the Strudel [shtroodel] family. They are going to help you learn to speak German.

Word lists

You will find a word list on every double page to tell you what the German words mean.

Guten Tag
gootn tahg

Hallo
hullaw

The little letters are to help you say the German words. Read them as if they were English words.

Ich bin
ikh bin
Rainer.
ryner

Einverstanden
ine fer shtanden

Nein
nine

Ja
yah

Word list

Guten Tag	hello
gootn tahg	
Hallo	hi
hullaw	
nein	no
nine	
ja	yes
yah	
ich bin	I am
ikh bin	
einverstanden	OK, I agree
ine fer shtanden	
du bist dran	your turn
doo bist dran	

The best way to find out how to say German words is to listen to a German person speaking. Some letters and sounds are a bit different from English. Here are some clues to help you.

When you see a "ch" in German, it is written "kh" in the little letters. Say this like the "h" in "huge". Say *ich* [ikh], which means "I". Some "ch"s are more like the "ch" in the Scottish word "loch".

Say "sch" like the "sh" sound in "show".

When you see one of these: ß, just say it like a double "s".

The "ei" in German sounds like "eye". Try saying *einverstanden* [ine fer shtanden] which means "OK".

The letter "j" in German sounds like the English "y".

Try saying out loud what each person on this page is saying.

See if you can find Josefina the mouse on each double page.

Games with word lists

You can play games with the word lists if you like. Here are some ideas.

1. Cover all the English words and see if you can say the English for each German word. Score a point for each one you can remember.

2. Time yourself and see if you can say the whole list more quickly next time.

3. Race a friend. The first one to say the English for each word scores a point. The winner is the one to score the most points.

4. Play all these games the other way around, saying the German for each English word.

Du bist dran
Look for the *du bist dran* [doo bist dran] boxes in this book. There is some-thing for you to do in each of them. *Du bist dran* means "your turn".

Look out for the joke bubbles on some of the pages.

3

Setting off

This is the Strudel family. They are getting ready to go away to the beach for a week. Unfortunately, everyone seems to have lost something.

Can you help by answering all of their questions? *Wo ist* [vaw ist] means "where is". Use the word list to know what the other words mean.

Everything can be found somewhere in the picture. Point to each missing object and say "it's there" in German. This is *da ist er* [dah ist air] if the object has *der* before it, or *da ist sie* [dah ist zee] if the object has *die* before it. Say *da ist es* [dah ist ess] if the object has *das* before it.

4

Word list

wo ist *vaw ist*	where is
da ist er *dah ist air*	he/it is there
da ist sie *dah ist zee*	she/it is there
da ist es *dah ist ess*	it is there
der Ball *dair bal*	ball
die Zeitung *dee tsy toong*	newspaper
die Angelrute *dee ang el roota*	fishing rod
der Korb *dair korp*	basket
der Regenschirm *dair ray gun sheerm*	umbrella
das Radio *dass rah dee aw*	radio
das Handtuch *dass rah dee aw*	towel
das Auto *dass owtaw*	car
Herr *hair*	Mr.
Oma *awma*	Granny

Names

Strudel *shtroodel*	Silvia *zilveeya*	Katja *katya*

Der, die and *das*

Der, die and *das* all mean "the", but in German all naming words (nouns) are either masculine, feminine or neuter. Masculine words have *der* before them, feminine words have *die* before them and neuter words have *das* before them.

When there is more than one thing (plural) the word for "the" is *die*.

5

Joke: What's yellow and black and wears a straw hat? A bee on holiday.

On the road

The Strudels quickly get lost. They've also lost some of their luggage on the way. Can you find it for them by following their route so far? Start at their house, which is *bei den Strudels* [by dane shtroodels] in German.

Now they want to see all the places on the word list on their way to the beach. Which way should they go? They can only pass each place once.

Word list

Remember, *der, die* and *das* all mean "the".

das Häuschen das hoyss khen	cottage
der Campingplatz dair kemping pluts	campsite
die Burg dee boorg	castle
das Café dass ka fay	café
der Bahnhof dair bahn hawf	station
der See dair zay	lake
der Wald dair valt	forest
der Bauernhof dair baowan hawf	farm
das blaue Haus dass blaowa howss	blue house
der Markt dair markt	market
der Strand dair shtrunt	beach

Can you find the windmill, the field, the church and the school on the map? Point to them and say their names out loud in German.

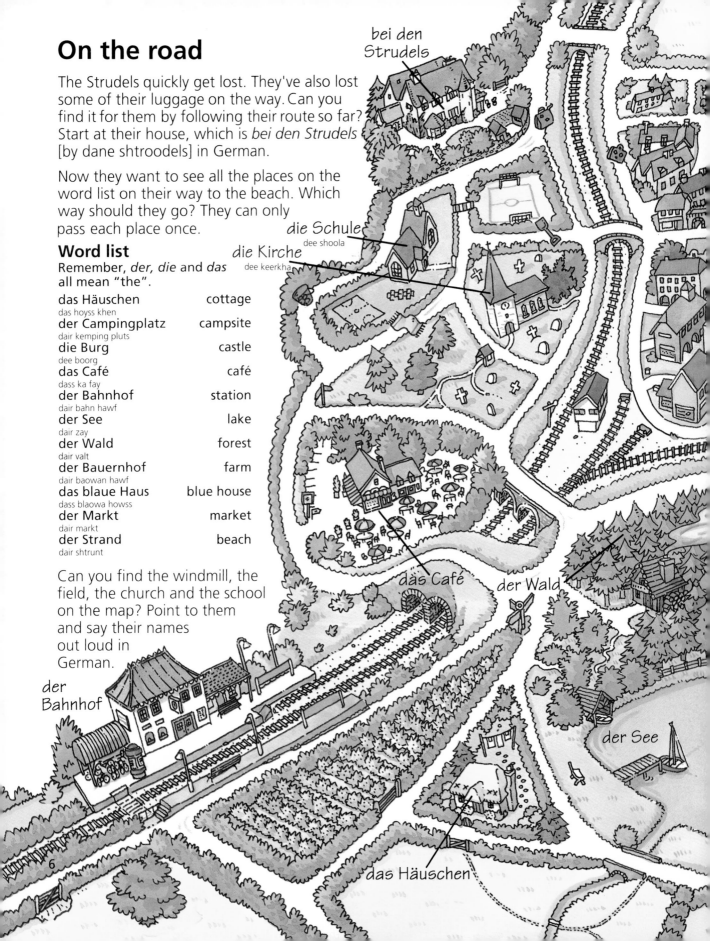

bei den Strudels

die Schule
dee shoola

die Kirche
dee keerkha

das Café

der Wald

der Bahnhof

der See

das Häuschen

6

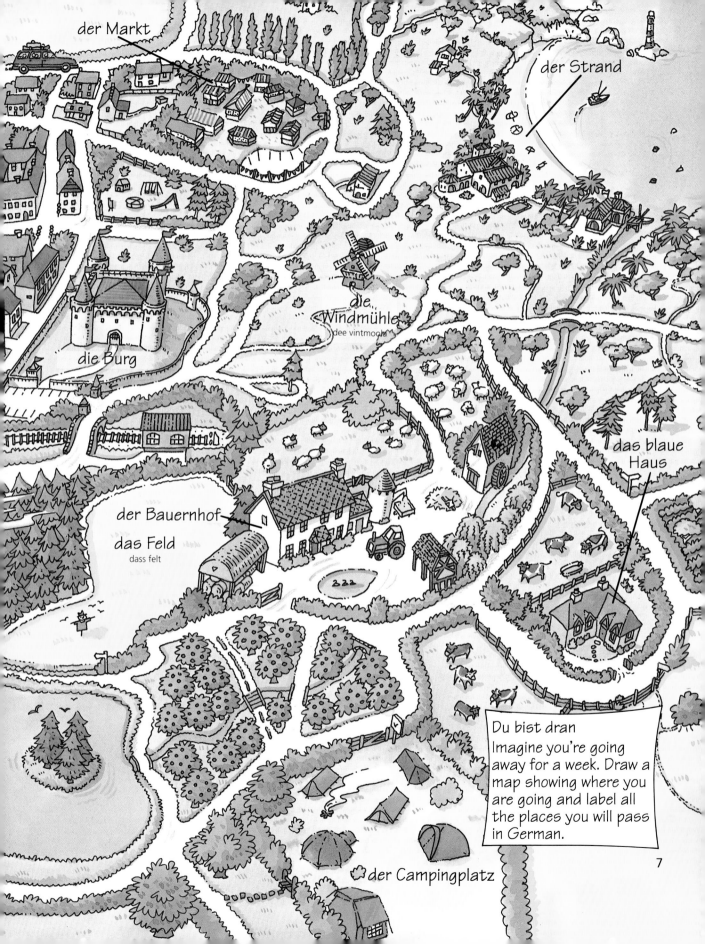

der Markt

der Strand

die Windmühle
dee vintmool

die Burg

der Bauernhof

das blaue Haus

das Feld
dass felt

Du bist dran

Imagine you're going away for a week. Draw a map showing where you are going and label all the places you will pass in German.

der Campingplatz

7

Counting game

Silvia, Markus, Katja and Uli set off to explore the countryside around the chalet where they are staying. In the forest they play a game to see who can spot the most wildlife. They write down how many of each thing they see.

Only one person has counted everything correctly. Can you see from their lists and the picture who it is?

Use the number key and word list to help you with the words.

Number key

eins ine ts	one	sechs zex	six
zwei tsvy	two	sieben zeebn	seven
drei dry	three	acht akht	eight
vier feer	four	neun noyn	nine
fünf foonf	five	zehn tsayn	ten

Names

Markus   Uli
mahrkoos   oolee

How many?

To ask "How many...are there?" in German, you say *Wieviele ... gibt es?* [vee feela gipt es]. To answer, you say *Es gibt* [ess gipt] and then the number of things. So to answer *Wieviele Katzen gibt es?*[vee feela katsn gipt ess] you would say *Es gibt zwei Katzen* [ess gipt tsvy katsn]. Can you answer the following questions in German?

Wieviele Bäume gibt es?

Wieviele Nester gibt es?

Wieviele Blumen gibt es?

Word list

Most naming words (nouns) change in the plural (when there is more than one) in German. *Der, die* and *das* are *die* in the plural.

die Kaninchen dee ka neen khen	rabbits	die Füchse dee fooksa	foxes
eine Maus ine a mouse	a mouse	die Schmetterlinge dee shmetterlinga	butterflies
die Mäuse dee moyza	mice	die Bäume dee boyma	trees
eine Katze,die Katzen ine a katsa, dee katsn	a cat,cats	die Blumen dee bloomn	flowers
die Hirsche dee heersha	stags	ein Nest,die Nester ine nest, dee nester	a nest,nests
die Vögel dee fergl	birds	wieviele vee feela	how many
die Schlangen dee shlungn	snakes	es gibt ess gipt	there is/are

Markus
sieben Vögel
acht Kaninchen
eine Maus
sechs Hirsche
vier Füchse
zwei Katzen
fünf Schmetterlinge
drei Schlangen

Katja
acht Vögel
sieben Kaninchen
zwei Mäuse
drei Hirsche
fünf Füchse
eine Katze
zehn Schmetterlinge
zwei Schlangen

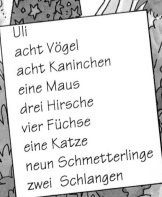

Uli
acht Vögel
acht Kaninchen
eine Maus
drei Hirsche
vier Füchse
eine Katze
neun Schmetterlinge
zwei Schlangen

Silvia
acht Vögel
acht Kaninchen
drei Mäuse
vier Hirsche
vier Füchse
eine Katze
sieben Schmetterlinge
zwei Schlangen

8 *Joke: What's the difference between a Siberian tiger and a Bengal tiger? 10 000km. (In Germany, distance is measured in km, not miles. To change miles to km, multiply by 8 and divide by 5.)

On the beach

On the first day at the beach, the Strudel children join a beach club. To help everyone get to know each other, they have all made name and age badges to wear.

Wie alt bist du? [vee ult bist doo] means "How old are you?" Katja answers, *Ich bin sieben Jahre alt* [ikh bin zeebn yahra ult], which means "I am seven years old".

Can you say in German what Uli, Markus and Silvia are saying? What would either of the twins say? Use the number list to help you.

Number list

eins* ine ts	one	sechs zex	six
zwei tsvy	two	sieben zeebn	seven
drei dry	three	acht akht	eight
vier feer	four	neun noyn	nine
fünf foonf	five	zehn tsayn	ten

*Eins only means "one" when you are counting.
"One year old" is ein Jahr alt [ine yahr ult].

Word list

wie alt bist du? how old are you?
vee ult bist doo

ich bin...Jahre alt   I'm...years old
ikh bin...yahra ult

wie heißt   what are you
du?   called?
vee hyste doo

ich heiße   I am called,
ikh hyssa   my name is

Wie alt bist du?

Markus
Ich bin 8
Jahre alt.

Ich bin 1
Jahr alt.

Elsa
Ich bin 6
Jahre alt.

Du bist dran

Make your own name and age badge in German. You will need: a piece of cardboard, a safety pin, sticky tape, a pen or pencil, scissors and a cup or mug.

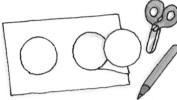

1. Draw a circle on the piece of cardboard, using the bottom of a cup (or any round object of the size you want your badge to be) to draw a perfect circle. Then cut it out.

2. Wie heißt du? [vee hyste doo]. Write on the circle what you are called and how old you are in German. Ich heiße [ikh hyssa] means "I am called".

Look at the picture to see how to write how old you are.

Ich heiße
Markus.
Ich bin 8
Jahre alt.

3. Stick a pin to the back of the circle with sticky tape. (Remember to only stick down one side of the pin so that it can still open).

Treasure hunt

Klaus [klowss], the leader of the beach club, has organized a treasure hunt. He has hidden the treasure in one of the red boxes in the picture.

Using the word and picture lists to help you, can you follow the clues below to find out which of the red boxes holds the treasure?

As you say each clue out loud in German, point to any of the red boxes you can see in that place. The treasure box is the only one which is in all the places on the list of clues.

Hinweise (Clues)
Auf dem Campingplatz
Hinter dem Zelt
Vor dem Baum
Neben dem Tor
Auf der Mauer
Unter dem Eimer

Word list

der Campingplatz dair kemping pluts	campsite
das Tor dass tawr	gate
der Baum dair baowm	tree
das Zelt dass tsellt	tent
die Mauer dee maower	wall
der Eimer dair eyemer	bucket

Picture list

hinter
hinter

auf
owf

unter
oonter

vor
fore

in
in

neben
naybn

Du bist dran

You could make up your own treasure hunt using German clues. Hide something and write down how to find it in German using Klaus's clues and/or any of the phrases below.

hinter dem Vorhang
hinter dame forehung

unter dem Tisch
oonter dame tish

vor dem Sofa
fore dame zawfah

unter dem Bett
oonter dame bet

auf dem Stein
owf dame shtyne

in dem Wäschekorb
in dame veshakorp

vor dem Spiegel
fore dame shpeegl

neben der Pflanze
naybn dair pfluntsa

hinter dem Papierkorb
hinter dame pupeerkorp

in dem Schrank
in dame shrunk

neben dem Fernseher
naybn dame fairn zayer

13

Guess who?

Klaus's next activity for the beach club is the Guess who? game. Everyone must pretend to be someone or something else. Klaus must guess what each child is pretending to be.

Can you see who is a mouse? Who is a king? *Ich bin* [ikh bin] means "I am". Using the word list to help you, say out loud in German what each child is thinking.

Ich bin ein Hund.

Ich bin ...

Ich bin ...

Ich bin ...

Ich bin ...

Ich bin ...

Du bist ein Mädchen.

Du bist eine Maus.

Du bist ein König.

Word list

ich bin ikh bin	I am	**ein Mädchen** ein mate khen	a girl
du bist doo bist	you are	**ein Junge** ein yoonga	a boy
ja yah	yes	**ein Mann** ine mun	a man
nein nine	no	**ein Vogel** ine fawgl	a bird
eine Katze ine a katza	a cat	**eine Königin** ine a kernig in	a queen
ein Pferd ine pfairt	a horse	**ein König** ine kernikh	a king
ein Hund ine hoont	a dog	**eine Maus** ine a mouse	a mouse
eine Frau ine a fraow	a woman		

14

Klaus has aready guessed what three people are. *Du bist* [doo bist] means "you are".

Can you say in German what he will say to all the others when he guesses what they are pretending to be?

Ich bin ...

Ich bin ...

Ich bin ...

Was sollte man
vass zollta mun
mit einer riesigen
mit ine a reezign
Maus nie tun?
mouse nee toon

Ich bin ...

Sich streiten.
zikh shtryten

Du bist eine Katze!

Ja, ich bin eine Katze.

Du bist dran

What are you?
You could play a Guess who? game in German with friends.

How to play:

Choose someone to be the first guesser. All the other players act out what they would like to be.

The guesser shouts out in German when he guesses someone, using *du bist* [doo bist] then what he thinks you are.

Say *ja* [yah] and then what you are in German if he is right. (Remember, *ich bin* means "I am"). You are then the next guesser.

Say *nein* [nine] if he is wrong and continue until someone is guessed correctly.

Once you have been a guesser, you must think of something else to be (or everyone will know at once what you are).

15

Joke: What must you never do with an enormous mouse? Argue.

Weather

Nobody in the Strudel family can agree about where to go on a rainy day. So Uli has stayed at the chalet with Karin and the twins while the others have all set off on different daytrips.

Which of the Strudels are joking when they phone Karin to tell her what the weather is like where they are? Use the word list to find out.

Can you say out loud in German what those who are joking should be saying to Karin?

Word list

wie ist das Wetter? vee ist dass vetter	what's the weather like?
es ist schön ess ist shern	it's fine
es regnet ess raygnet	it's raining
es ist kalt ess ist kullt	it's cold
es ist sehr warm ess ist zair vahrm	it's hot
es ist windig ess ist vindikh	it's windy
es schneit ess shnite	it's snowing
hier here	here

16

Names

Karin	Helga
kahrin	hellga

Du bist dran

Wie ist das Wetter? [vee ist dass vetter]. What's the weather like where you are at the moment? Can you say it in German?

You could write a postcard in German telling someone what the weather is like. Use the word lists, the pictures and the postcard Silvia has written to her friend, Helga, to see how to say all the words you need.

If you are writing to a boy or man you write lieber.

This means "How are you?"

Liebe Helga,
Wie geht's?
Es ist sehr warm hier.
Viele Grüße,
Silvia.

This means "love from". German people often write this at the end of a card or letter.

Word list

lieber/liebe	dear..
leeber,leeba	
wie geht's?	how are you?
vee gates	
sehr	very
zair	
viele Grüße	love from
feela grewssa	

Silvia's body game

When everyone returns to the house, the rain is still pouring down. Silvia has made up a game for everyone to play.

Why don't you make Silvia's body game and play it too?

You will need: a dice, paper, pencils or felt tip pens.

Du bist dran.

der Körper

This is the shape you start with.

·	ein Fuß
··	eine Hand
·.·	ein Arm
::	ein Bein
::.	der Kopf
:::	der Körper

The idea of the game is to be the first to complete a drawing of a person. Take turns throwing the dice. You must throw a 6 and shout out *der Körper* [dair kerper] to start. You can then draw the body.

Use the key above to see which numbers you must throw to add the other parts.

Say the name of each body part in German as you draw it. If you already have the part for any number you throw, pass the dice to the next player. (Remember that you need 2 arms, legs, feet and hands.)

You cannot add hands and feet before the arms and legs.

The first player to complete their person shouts out *der Mensch* [dair mensh], and is the winner. *Ich habe gewonnen* [ikh hahba gavonnen] means "I've won".

Der Mensch! Ich habe gewonnen.

Picture list

der Mensch
dair mensh
person

der Kopf
dair kopf
head

die Hand
dee hunt
hand

der Arm
dair arm
arm

der Körper
dair kerper
body

das Bein
dass bine
leg

der Fuß
dair fooss
foot

Making faces

You can play the same game with faces. Cut out lots of eyes, eyebrows, noses, ears and mouths from old magazines. Stick these on paper plates to make up your faces.

You will need: paper plates, old magazines, scissors, glue and felt tip pens.

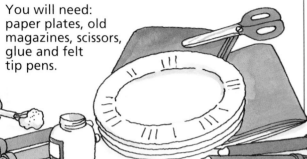

Picture list

 die Haare
dee hahra
hair

 das Auge
dass owga
eye

 die Augenbraue
dee owgn braowa
eyebrow

 die Nase
dee nahza
nose

 der Mund
dair moont
mouth

 das Ohr
dass or
ear

die Haare

Play in the same way as the body game. You must throw a 6 and shout out *die Haare* [dee hahra] to start. Draw on the hair with felt tips.

Check the number on the dice against the key below to see which parts you can then stick on. Remember to say the name of each part in German as you stick it on.

der Mund
die Nase
eine Augenbraue
ein Ohr
ein Auge
die Haare

Der Kopf! Ich habe gewonnen.

The first one to complete their head with hair, 2 eyes, 2 eyebrows, 2 ears, a nose and a mouth shouts *der Kopf* [dair kopf], which means "the head", and is the winner.

Song

Here is a song about faces and bodies to sing in German. Point to each part of the body as you sing about it. You can find the tune on page 32.

Kopf und Schultern, Knie und Zehe, Knie und Zehe,
kopf oont shooltern k neeya oont tsaya k neeya oont tsaya
Kopf und Schultern, Knie und Zehe, Knie und Zehe,
kopf oont shooltern k neeya oont tsaya k neeya oont tsaya
Augen, Nase, Ohren und Mund,
owgn nahza aw ren oont moont
Kopf und Schultern, Knie und Zehe, Knie und Zehe.
kopf oont shooltern k neeya oont tsaya k neeya oont tsaya

Head and shoulders, knees and toes, knees and toes,
Head and shoulders, knees and toes, knees and toes,
Eyes, nose, ears and mouth,
Head and shoulders, knees and toes, knees and toes.

Car game

The next day dawns bright and sunny and the Strudels pile into the car to go to the fair along the coast. It is a long drive so they play a guessing game to pass the time.

The game is to give clues to somewhere and everyone has to guess where this place is.

Es gibt [ess gipt] means "there is" or "there are".

Frau Strudel starts. She says that at the place she is thinking of *Es gibt das Meer, Sand, Steine* [ess gipt das mair zunt shtyna]. This means "there is the sea, sand, rocks...". Markus guesses *Es ist der Strand* [ess ist dair shtrunt] which means "it's the beach". He is right so now it is his turn.

Use the word list to help you see what the others are thinking of. Say the clues out loud, then shout out the right answer from the answer list.

Names

Frau Strudel   Mrs. Strudel
fraow shtroodel

Du bist dran
You can play this game too. Just say *es gibt* [ess gipt] and a few of the words on the word list to describe the place you are thinking about and wait until someone guesses correctly - in German of course.

20

Es gibt das Meer, Sand, Steine...

Es ist der Strand!

Es gibt Boote, das Meer, Matrosen...

Es gibt Pralinen, Geld, eine Theke...

Es gibt
Autos, Straßen,
Gebäude...

Word list

es gibt	there is, there are	die Blumen	flowers
ess gipt		*dee bloomn*	
es ist	it is	die Pralinen	chocolates
ess ist		*dee prah leenen*	
das Meer	sea	die Matrosen	sailors
dass mair		*dee matrawzen*	
das Geld	money	die Schaukeln	swings
dass gelt		*dee shaowkeln*	
der Sand	sand	die Vögel	birds
dair zunt		*dee fergl*	
die Theke	(shop,store) counter	die Steine	rocks
dee tayka		*dee shtyna*	
die Bänke	benches	die Straßen	streets
dee benka		*dee shtrahssen*	
die Boote	boats	die Autos	car
dee bawta		*dee owtaws*	
die Gebäude	buildings	die Bäume	trees
dee geboyda		*dee boyma*	

Remember that in German, naming words (nouns) usually change when they mean more than one of something (plural). Most words on this list are plurals. You can see how to say the words for one of each thing (singular) on pages 30 and 31.

Es gibt
Schaukeln,
Bänke...

E

Answer list

das Geschäft	shop, store
dass gesheft	
der Wald	forest
dair valt	
der Strand	beach
dair shtrunt	
die Stadt	town
dee shtut	
der Park	park
dair park	
der Hafen	port
dair hahfen	

Es gibt
Bäume, Blumen,
Vögel...

Was ist groß,
vass ist grawss
grau und macht
graow oont mahkht
"ooooo"?
ooo

Ein
ine
Ele-phantom.
el lay funtawm

F

21

Joke: What's big, grey and goes "ooooo"? An ele-phantom.

Funny shapes

When they reach the fair, the Strudels go into the Hall of Mirrors. The mirrors make people look very different from their normal shape and size.

Silvia's reflection is too big. Markus says, *Sie ist zu groß* [zee ist tsoo grawss], which means "she is too big".

Can you say what is wrong with each person's reflection? Use the word list to find out the words for tall, small, fat and thin.

If it is a boy or a man, say *er ist* [air ist]. If it is a girl or a woman, say *sie ist* [zee ist].

Sie ist zu groß.

22

Picture list

Describing words (adjectives) in German usually change their spelling when they come before a naming word (noun). On this page they don't.

klein klyne	small, short	dick dick	fat
groß grawss	big, tall	dünn doon	thin

Word list

ich bin ikh bin	I am	sie ist zee ist	she is
zu tsoo	too	er ist air ist	he is

Was ist
vass ist
schwarzweiß und
shvarts vice oont
sehr laut?
zair lout

Ein Pinguin,
ine pinggoo een
der Trompete
dair trompayta
spielt.
shpeelt

Du bist dran

Are you tall or small? To answer, say *ich bin* [ikh bin] which means "I am" and then the right word from the word list.

Describe your family too, using *er ist* [air ist] for males and *sie ist* [zee ist] for females.

Ich bin klein.

23

Joke: What's black and white and very noisy? A penguin playing the trumpet. (In German, you don't say the "and" in "black and white". It's just *schwarzweiß*.)

Hot work

On the way home from the fair, the Strudels' car breaks down. Setting off on foot, they all realize how hungry or thirsty they are.

Can you see which roads Karin and the twins, Josefina, Oma and Herr Strudel should take to get what they want?

Ich habe Hunger [ikh hahba hoonger] means "I'm hungry". *Ich habe Durst* [ikh hahba doorst] means "I'm thirsty".

Ich habe Hunger.

Ich habe Durst.

Ich habe Hunger.

Ich habe Durst.

A

B

C

D

E

F

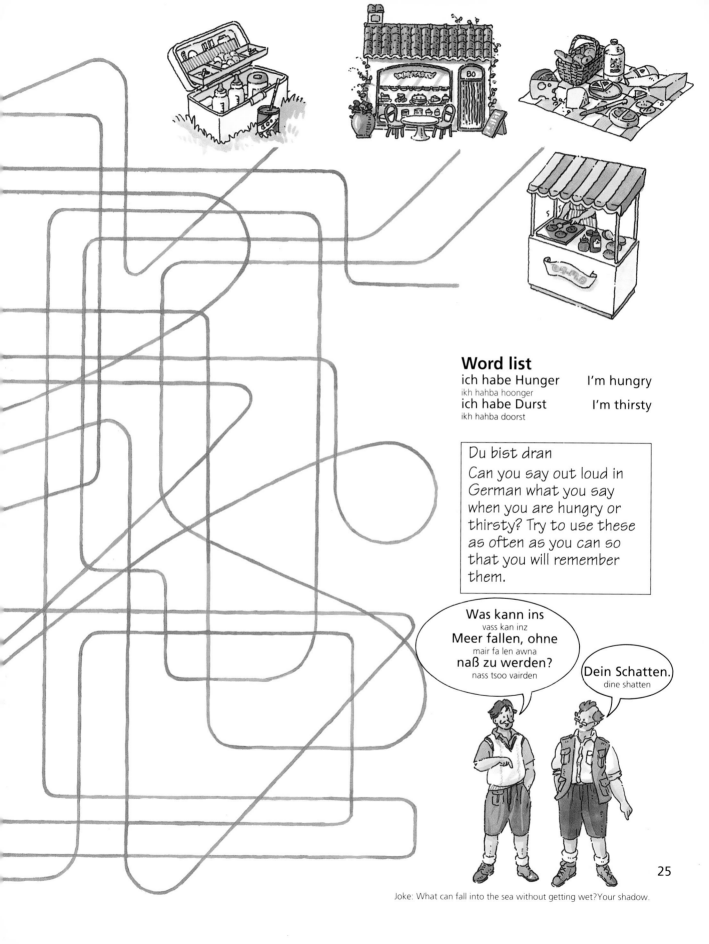

Word list

ich habe Hunger	I'm hungry
ikh hahba hoonger	
ich habe Durst	I'm thirsty
ikh hahba doorst	

Du bist dran
Can you say out loud in German what you say when you are hungry or thirsty? Try to use these as often as you can so that you will remember them.

Was kann ins
vass kan inz
Meer fallen, ohne
mair fa len awna
naß zu werden?
nass tsoo vairden

Dein Schatten.
dine shatten

25

Joke: What can fall into the sea without getting wet? Your shadow.

Snapshots

The twins have got hold of some of Markus's photographs and have torn them into pieces. Oma Strudel has offered to stick the mixed-up pieces back together. Markus has written a note to help her. Read it to see what Silvia, Onkel Helmut and Tante Ilse are wearing in the photographs. *Trägt* [traykt] after someone's name means "is wearing" in German. Can you help Oma see which six pieces belong to each photograph?

Markus's note

Onkel Helmut trägt einen Mantel, ein Hemd, eine Hose und Schuhe.

Silvia trägt einen Badeanzug, einen Hut und Stiefel.

Tante Ilse trägt eine Sonnenbrille, einen Rock, einen Pullover und Socken.

Use the word list to read out loud in German what each person is wearing.

Word list

schade! shahda	what a pity!
..trägt.. traykt	..is wearing..
ich trage ikh trahga	I am wearing
ein Rock* ine rock	a skirt
ein Pullover* ine pull awver	a pullover
ein Badeanzug* ine bahda an tsoog	a swimsuit
eine Sonnenbrille zonnen brilla	sunglasses
eine Hose ine a hawza	trousers
ein Mantel* ine muntle	a coat
ein Hemd* ine hemt	a shirt
ein Hut* ine hoot	a hat
Socken zokken	socks
Schuhe shooa	shoes
Stiefel shteefle	boots
und oont	and
was trägst du? vass traykst doo	what are you wearing?

*Did you notice the word *einen* before some of the words in Markus's note? The word for "a" changes from *ein* to *einen* with *der* (masculine) words. These are marked * on the word list.

Names

Onkel Helmut onkel helmoot	Uncle Helmut

Du bist dran

Was trägst du? [vass traykst doo]. What are you wearing? Say *ich trage* [ikh trahga] and then your clothes. Can you describe what your family or friends are wearing? Here are some more clothes words that you may need.

ein Kleid ine klyte	a dress
ein T-Shirt ine tee shirt	a T-Shirt
Shorts shorts	shorts

27

Joke: What's green and goes tic-toc? A clockwork cucumber.

Going home

It's time for the Strudels to say goodbye to all the people they have met at the beach.

On the way home, they stop to buy little presents and souvenirs. Uli already knows what he wants to buy - the green flippers.

Can you see what everyone else would like? Use the word list to help you say in German how each person will ask for what he or she wants. Look at the guide opposite to see how to say the describing words on their own.

Word list

ich möchte...	I would like...
ikh merkhta	
die grünen Flossen	the green flippers
dee grewnen flossen	
die grüne Marionette	the green puppet
dee grewna marionetta	
die braune Marionette	the brown puppet
dee browna marionetta	
das lila Portemonnaie	the purple(money)purse
dass leelah port monnay	
die weißen Stiefel	the white boots
dee vyssen shteefle	
die gelben Blumen	the yellow flowers
dee gelben bloomn	
die roten Blumen	the red flowers
dee rawtn bloomn	
die blaue Tasche	the blue bag
dee blaowa tasha	
die schwarze Trommel	the black drum
dee shvahrtsa trommel	
bitte	please
bitta	
Auf Wiedersehen	goodbye
owf veederzane	

28

Song

Here is a song about a rainbow to sing in German.
You can see what all the words mean on page 32.

Rot und ro-sa und gelb und grün, vi-o-lett, li-la und blau,
rawt oont raw za oont gelp oont grewn vee aw let lee lah oont blaow

bun-ter Re-gen-bo-gen, schö-ner Bo-gen, mei-ne Welt'st nicht grau. Im
boon ter ray gn baw gn sher ner baw gn my na velts nikht graow im

Som-mer ist es grün, die Fel-der voll-er gelb, und die Wol-ken am Him-mel weiß,
zom mer ist ess grewn dee fell der foll er gelp oont dee vol ken am him mel vice

ro-te Ro-sen blü-hen, Far-ben glü-hen, und es wächst viel Mais.
raw ta raw zen blew en far ben glew en oont ess vext feel mice

Du bist dran
Which object would you most like to have? Can you ask for it in German?

Guide

rot
rawt
blau
blaow
gelb
gelp
rosa
rawza
grün
grewn
braun
brown
lila
leelah
schwarz
shvahrts
weiß
vice

Did you notice that the describing words on the word list are different from the ones above? In German, describing words (adjectives) usually change their spelling when they come before naming words (nouns).

29

Word list

Here is a list of all the German words and phrases** used in this book in alphabetical order. You can use the list either to check quickly what a word means or to test yourself. Cover up any German or English word or phrase and see if you can say its translation. Remember that most words change slightly when you are talking about more than one thing (plural).

acht	akht	eight
Angelrute (die)	ang el roota	fishing rod
Arm (der)	arm	arm
auf	owf	on (top of)
Auf Wiedersehen	owf veederzane	goodbye
Auge (das)	owga	eye
Augenbraue (die)	owgn braowa	eyebrow
Auto (das),	owtaw,	car,
Autos (die)	owtaws	cars
Badeanzug (der)	bahda an tsoog	swimsuit
Bahnhof (der)	bahn hawf	station
Ball (der)	bal	ball
Bank (die)	bank	bench
Bänke (die)	benka	benches
Bauernhof (der)	baowan hawf	farm
Baum (der)	baowm	tree
Bäume (die)	boyma	trees
bei den Strudels	by dane	(at) the
	shtroodels	Strudels' home
Bein (das)	bine	leg
Bett (das)	bet	bed
bitte	bitta	please
blau	blaow	blue
Blume, Blumen (die)	blooma, bloomn	flower (s)
Boot (das),	bawt,	boat,
Boote (die)	bawta	boats
braun	brown	brown
Burg (die)	boorg	castle
Café (das)	ka fay	café
Campingplatz (der)	kemping pluts	campsite
da ist er, sie, es	dah ist air,zee,ess	there it is
der, die, das	dair, dee, dass	the
dick	dick	fat
drei	dry	three
du bist	doo bist	you are
du bist dran	doo bist dran	your turn
dünn	doon*	thin
Eimer (der)	eyemer	bucket
ein, eine, einen	ine, ine a, ine n	a/an/one
eins	ine ts	one
einverstanden	ine fer shtanden	OK, agreed

er heißt	air hyste	he is called
er ist	air ist	he is
es gibt	ess gipt	there is/there are
es ist	ess ist	it is
es ist kalt	ess ist kullt	it's cold
es ist schön	ess ist shern	it's fine
es ist sehr warm	ess ist zair vahrm	it's hot
es ist windig	ess ist vindikh	it's windy
es regnet	ess raygnet	it's raining
es schneit	ess shnite	it's snowing
Feld (das)	felt	field
Fernseher (der)	fairn zayer	television
Flossen (die)	flossen	flippers
Frau (die)	fraow	Mrs., woman
Fuchs (der)	fooks*	fox
Füchse (die)	fooksa*	foxes
fünf	foonf*	five
Fuß (der)	fooss	foot
Gebäude (das),(die)	geboyda	building, building
gelb	gelp	yellow
Geld (das)	gelt	money
Geschäft (das)	gesheft	shop, store
groß	grawss	big, tall
grün	grewn	green
Guten Abend	gootn ah bnd	good evening
Guten Tag	gootn tahg	hello
Haare (die)	hahra	hair
Hafen (der)	hahfen	port
Hallo	hullaw	hi
Hand (die)	hunt	hand
Handtuch (das)	hunt tookh	towel
Haus (das)	howss	house
Häuschen (das)	hoyss khen	cottage
Hemd (das)	hemt	shirt
Herr	hair	Mr.
hier	here	here
hinter	hinter	behind
Hirsch (der)	heersh	stag
Hirsche (die)	heersha	stags
Hose (die)	hawza	trousers
Hund (der)	hoont*	dog
Hut (der)	hoot	hat
ich bin	ikh bin	I am
ich habe Durst	ikh hahba doorst	I'm thirsty
ich habe	ikh hahba	I've won
gewonnen	gavonnen	
ich habe Hunger	ikh hahba hoonger*	I'm hungry
ich heiße	ikh hyssa	I am called
ich möchte	ikh merkhta	I would like
ich spreche	ikh shprekha	I speak
Deutsch	doytsh	German
ich trage	ikh trahga	I am wearing
in	in	in
ja	yah	yes

30

* The 'u' sound in these words is like the 'u' in 'put'.
**Except those in the jokes and songs, which are translated on the pages or on the answer page.

Jahre alt	yahra ult	*years old*
Junge (der)	yoonga*	*boy*
Kaninchen (das),(die)	ka neen khn	*rabbit, rabbits*
Katze, Katzen (die)	katsa, katsn	*cat, cats*
Kirche (die)	keerkha	*church*
Kleid (das)	klyte	*dress*
klein	klyne	*small, short*
König (der)	kernikh	*king*
Königin (die)	kernig in	*queen*
Kopf (der)	kopf	*head*
Korb (der)	korp	*basket*
Körper (der)	kerper	*body*
lieber, liebe	leeber, leeba	*dear*
lila	leelah	*purple*
Mädchen (das)	mate khen	*girl*
Mann (der)	mun	*man*
Mantel (der)	muntle	*coat*
Marionette (die)	marionetta	*puppet*
Markt (der)	markt	*market*
Matrose (der)	matrawza	*sailor*
Matrosen (die)	matrawzen	*sailors*
Mauer (die)	maower	*wall*
Maus, Mäuse (die)	mouse, moyza	*mouse, mice*
Meer (das)	mair	*sea*
Mensch (der)	mensh	*person*
Mund (der)	moont*	*mouth*
Nase (die)	nahza	*nose*
neben	naybn	*beside*
nein	nine	*no*
Nest (das)	nest	*nest*
Nester (die)	nester	*nests*
neun	noyn	*nine*
Ohr (das)	or	*ear*
Ohren (die)	aw ren	*ears*
Oma (die)	awma	*grandma*
Papierkorb (der)	pupeerkorp	*wastepaper basket*
Park (der)	park	*park*
Pferd (das)	pfairt	*horse*
Pflanze (die)	pfluntsa	*plant*
Pralinen (die)	prah leenan	*chocolates*
Portemonnaie (das)	port monnay	*(money)purse*
Pullover (der)	pull awver	*pullover*
Radio (das)	rah dee aw	*radio*
Regenschirm (der)	ray gun sheerm	*umbrella*
Rock (der)	rock	*skirt*
rosa	rawza	*pink*
rot	rawt	*red*
Sand (der)	zunt	*sand*
schade!	shahda	*what a pity!*
Schaukel (die)	shaowkel	*swing*
Schaukeln (die)	shaowkeln	*swings*
Schlange(die)	shlunga	*snake,*
Schlangen (die)	shlungn	*snakes*
Schrank (der)	shrunk	*cupboard*
Schmetterling (der)	shmetterling	*butterfly*
Schmetterlinge (die)	shmetterlinga	*butterflies*
Schuh (der)	shoo	*shoe*
Schule (die)	shoola	*school*
schwarz	shvahrts	*black*
sechs	zex	*six*
See (der)	zay	*lake*
sehr	zair	*very*
Shorts (die)	shorts	*shorts*
sieben	zeebn	*seven*
sie ist	zee ist	*she is*
Socke (die)	zokka	*sock*
Sofa (das)	zawfah	*sofa*
Sonnenbrille (die)	zonnen brilla	*(a pair of) sunglasses*
Spiegel (der)	shpeegl	*mirror*
Spiel (das), Spiele(die)	shpeel, shpeela	*game, games*
Stadt (die)	shtut	*town*
Stein (der), Steine(die)	shtyne, shtyna	*rock, rocks*
Stiefel (der)	shteefle	*boot*
Strand (der)	shtrunt	*beach*
Straße (die)	shtrahssa	*street*
Straßen (die)	shtrahssan	*streets*
Tasche (die)	tasha	*bag*
Theke (die)	tayka	*(shop)counter*
Tisch (der)	tish	*table*
Tor (das)	tawr	*gate*
..trägt	traykt	*.. is wearing*
Trommel (die)	trommel	*drum*
T-Shirt (das)	tee shirt	*T-shirt*
und	oont*	*and*
unter	oonter*	*under*
viele Grüße	feela grewssa	*love from*
vier	feer	*four*
Vogel (der), Vögel(die)	fawgl, fergl	*bird, birds*
vor	fore	*in front of*
Vorhang (der)	fore hung	*curtain*
Wald (der)	valt	*forest*
Wäschekorb (der)	veshakorp	*laundry basket*
was ist	vass ist	*what is*
was trägst du?	vass traykst doo	*what are you wearing?*
weiß	vice	*white*
wie alt bist du?	vee ult bist doo	*how old are you?*
wie geht's?	vee gates	*how are you?*
wie heißt du?	vee hyste doo	*what are you called?*
wie ist das Wetter?	vee ist dass vetter	*what's the weather like?*
wieviele?	vee feela	*how many?*
Windmühle (die)	vintmoola	*windmill*
wo ist	vaw ist	*where is*
zehn	tsayn	*ten*
Zeitung (die)	tsy toong*	*newspaper*
Zelt (das)	tsellt	*tent*
zu	tsoo	*too*
zwei	tsvy	*two*

Answers

PAGE 6-7

PAGE 8-9

Uli has counted correctly.
Es gibt sieben Bäume.
Es gibt ein Nest.
Es gibt zehn Blumen.

PAGE 10-11

Markus is saying *Ich bin acht Jahre alt.*
Uli is saying *Wie alt bist du?*
Silvia is saying *Ich bin sieben Jahre alt.*
Either of the twins would say *Ich bin ein Jahr alt.*

PAGE 12-13

The box that Uli finds is in the right place.

PAGE 14-15

Klaus will say:
Du bist ein Hund; Du bist eine Katze; Du bist ein Junge; Du bist eine Frau; Du bist eine Königin; Du bist ein Pferd; Du bist ein Vogel; Du bist ein Mann.

PAGE 16-17

Oma is joking. She should say *Es ist windig.*

Herr Strudel is joking. He should say *Es regnet.*

Onkel Helmut is joking. He should say *Es ist sehr warm.*

PAGE 18-19

PAGE 20-21

A. *Es ist der Strand.* D. *Es ist die Stadt.*
B. *Es ist der Hafen.* E. *Es ist der Park.*
C. *Es ist das Geschäft.* F. *Es ist der Wald.*

PAGE 24-25

Karin and the twins take road F,
Josefina takes road C,
Oma takes road E,
Herr Strudel takes road B.

PAGE 26-27

Silvia: F G I M O R
Tante Ilse: B D E J L Q
Onkel Helmut: A C H K N P

PAGE 28-29

Katja: *Ich möchte das lila Portemonnaie.*
Tante Ilse: *Ich möchte die blaue Tasche.*
Herr Strudel: *Ich möchte die roten Blumen.*
Frau Strudel: *Ich möchte die gelben Blumen.*
Onkel Helmut: *Ich möchte die schwarze Trommel.*
Markus: *Ich möchte die braune Marionette.*
Silvia: *Ich möchte die grüne Marionette.*
Oma Strudel: *Ich möchte die weißen Stiefel.*

Here are the words of the song in English:

Red and pink and yellow and green,
Violet, purple and blue,
Colourful rainbow, beautiful arc,
My world's not grey.
In summer it is green
The fields full of yellow
And the clouds in the sky are white.
Red roses are blooming
Colours are glowing
And there's lots of corn growing.